Her Colored Scars

Written By: J. A. Bishop

Cover Design by Islam Farid
www.islamfarid.net

Her Colored Scars

Table of contents

Dear Readers,

I grew up quiet, secluded in my own world only embracing the few friends I let inside along with my family. Everyone and everything else I feared.

With time you grow up though, you change. You let more people inside your life, little by little. Then you realize those people don't stay and the love you let in, doesn't last. After all of that you're left remembering why you feared everything that was outside of your bubble.

I wrote, Her Colored Scars for myself, but in hopes that readers around the world could relate. Sometimes, words are the only way to express ourselves and bringing those words to life on paper makes our hearts a little lighter.

So, if you think you're alone in this world with different emotions running through your mind, body and soul, rest assure that you will never be alone.

-Jennifer

Her Colored Scars

I have colored scars,

ones you can't touch with your fingertips.

Scars left over from people who

thought they were stronger than me.

For this I am not ashamed.

These are my colors,

these are my scars.

J. A. Bishop

Her

Innocence

I've been innocent, but if you ask I have sinned. I've been the forgiver. Still, I can remember the days where I was done wrong. Some days, I'm the grudge holder. I've been the believer and the skeptic, I am human. I've been weak, when I should've been strong.

Don't judge me for I am me.

Her Colored Scars

Like a flower
in the middle of a forest,
blooming alone.
I too have always been the one
standing by herself away
from the crowd to have
room to breathe and grow.

What I wouldn't give
to be little again.
To be carefree.
Swinging back and forth
on the school playground,
trying to touch the sky.

Can you remember
being innocent?
Sitting Indian-Style
on your bedroom floor
braiding your friend's hair,
listening to CDs.
Talking about what it
would be like to be
thirty, flirty and fabulous.

I watched the lighting bugs fly midair looking for mates during the twilight hours of a hot humid summer day.

Young memories of nostalgia days at my grandparents' house.

Writing from your heart
is the purest act of rawness.
That doesn't mean that everyone needs to
know everything kept within your heart.
Some things you're allowed to keep
concealed.

Many people might've thought I was naïve, going into the world thinking that it wasn't going to hurt me, and not let me down. Truth is, the world has been wonderful to me. It's the people in it who have hurt me in unexplainable ways.

Innocent kisses
are the ones that
get replayed in our minds.
The ones that give us
that fluttery feeling
when we think about it.

Imagine having to fight for the most faultless part of a relationship. Hand holding down the street, a simple peck on the cheek, a slight touch on the back. Perhaps, even a heavy I love you, so low in fear that someone that disapproves over hears. Imagine having to fight to show your love every day.

Would you want to live like that?

 Then why do you expect us to?

Her Colored Scars

Careful playing
hide-and-seek in
someone else's eyes.
They might get tired
of playing and their
will be no one else to find you.

You should love yourself just the way you are. You're blessed not to be like the other girls in your class. Blonde hair and blue eyes doesn't make you prettier than your friends, a small waist doesn't get you a date to the dance and you should never be ashamed of who you are.

If only I could tell my younger self this.

Her Colored Scars

I love regardless of distance.

I Choose love over it all.

I see through the miles,

the trees and any obstacles.

A home so far away

just like Heaven.

A place you can't see,

but you know you belong.

Acceptance of who I was
never came from some of my family.
I was loved, but only for the person
they believed me to be. In their eyes,
I was still the little girl with the
long brown hair, holding her head down
never saying anything.

Her Colored Scars

They don't know
how hard I tried,
how hard I prayed
that every night
the Lord would
forgive me for who
I gave my heart to.

I could feel it deep within
my bones though, he already
knew who carved their name
in my heart for eternity.

Isn't it funny?

How your parents made life seem somewhat bearable. Despite all of that now, you know they were just pretending.

Her Colored Scars

There was always
a gathering on
the front porch
where the wind met
the wind chimes
and us children gossiped
about our school days
along the steps.

I don't think front porch
conversations like that
happen anymore.

Coming out of the closet

is like coming out

of the biggest storm of your life.

No matter the size of the storm you're still

blessed with a beautiful rainbow.

There's always an innocence in
meeting someone new.
A clean slate, a new beginning, a
chance to do everything all over
again for the first time.

Love use to be foreign to me.

A language that I didn't know.

Simply because I read

about loving women out of books.

Her Colored Scars

Friends, that's what we were.
Friends that spoke like lovers,
and that was just enough
to get us in trouble.

You can't play innocent
for the things you
have already learned.
Eventually all bad intentions
are brought to light.

Her Colored Scars

Your voice echoes
back to me,
like two teenagers
exploring a cave that
they just discovered
after a night of breaking curfew.

J. A. Bishop

We're all just adults

that's still a kid at heart,

trying to learn how to freeze time.

Her Colored Scars

Color my world like
crayons scribbled on a wall
when you were younger
and didn't fear
coloring outside the lines.

From moments of neglect and verbal abuse, there's nothing else to gain from loving you. You will forever be a lesson of a lifetime of how one should not love.

Her Colored Scars

We give up
so much of ourselves
when we cross paths
with the wrong person.

J. A. Bishop

My favorite color

is neither pink nor blue.

You shouldn't teach

that a color should be

based upon a gender.

Her Colored Scars

Sometimes you just need
to hear you're wanted.
That's not neediness,
it's a level of comfort.

Imagine how simpler life would be if people would grant answers before questions even spilled out of our mouths. No deception and no need for overthinking. Just an honest person baring their true intentions.

Her Colored Scars

I grew up living within
the straight lines never
wandering outside
to worry my parents.
It was during my
adolescent years that
I crossed the lines for
a better understanding
of this thing we call life.

To be young and not love

would be a complete waste.

What good is the heart if you won't love?

Her Colored Scars

I remember
when the rain would
pour down on me
and there wasn't
anything to wash away.
It was just me and the rain.

J. A. Bishop

If only there was a way
to travel back in time to
believe in myself sooner,
I could live out my dreams longer.

Her Colored Scars

Like a designer dress
in a window that
you could only admire.
I wasn't meant to be touched
with unclean hands.

It's amazing

how much pain

my smile hid at a young age.

Her Colored Scars

She was a leaf
falling from a tree
down at my feet.

Waiting for me
to pick her up,
and explore her colors,
along with the creases
on her body, front and back.

The wind could've blown her anywhere
but here she was at my feet.

It was beautiful,

the days she let me be myself

with no judgement.

Her Colored Scars

You held the first place
in my heart.
To some, there really
isn't a higher honor than that.

Love was love.

Love won

above all else.

It didn't matter

if love was

heterosexual,

homosexual or bisexual.

When you love

with no hesitation with no fear.

You win.

Her Colored Scars

If only the world
was turned upside
down when we fell.
We would land
among the cotton candy
skies and white clouds.

I don't think anyone
would be afraid of falling then.

It's too soon for you

to experience my lips on your body.

Perhaps we will start

with my words being whispered in your ear.

Her Colored Scars

She craved
my innocence
and I craved
her wild heart.

J. A. Bishop

To be born with a pulse

is to be born with a reason.

Her Colored Scars

You can reclaim your innocence after
fighting to protect your peace.

Innocence is never truly lost.

I have wandering feet

that have taken paths along the wrong souls.

It's there, I found love can both hurt and heal you.

Her Colored Scars

I use all my fall lashes
for wishes that you will be mine.

I wanted to say a thousand words to you, but my walls were up, and my words remained silent.

I couldn't knock them down in hopes you weren't like the rest and wouldn't leave.

Not yet anyways.

Her Colored Scars

She had a way about her.

The flowers in fields
would sway with no wind.

J. A. Bishop

Look for the love

that you believed in

when you were still young

and didn't know bad people existed.

Her Colored Scars

You can give
until you have nothing left.
Still people will
say you didn't give enough.

I let my thoughts wander,
but why do they always run
back to you.

Her Colored Scars

We barely spoke
but when our
eyes connected
it's like we had been
speaking for years.

J. A. Bishop

To you my body was fat.

A canvas with scars and blemishes.

To me,

It's the place that carries my soul

and provides endless love.

Her Colored Scars

I've always
been too fragile
in a world filled with
careless handlers.

Why is it people spend time

searching for silver coins to pick up

when there's pennies everywhere.

Don't they know that

every coin holds its own unique value.

Her Colored Scars

If people would quit
promising not to leave.

I would quit
expecting them to stay.

Do not tell me

how brave I am

for my sexuality

and then judge me

when it's in your face.

Her Colored Scars

At the end of the day
I must come to terms
with all the thoughts
I have, are mine.

The good and the bad.

J. A. Bishop

A red heart

I was born with

now splattered

with hues of black, blue and shades purple

for the beating it has taken.

Her Colored Scars

I was once scared
to live not knowing
what was ahead of me in life.

How silly of me
not to know that
I was protected by the unseen.

J. A. Bishop

Her

Suffering

You took your love and abandoned me.

Gifting me with a lifetime of words that needed to be unwrapped. Words that needed to be heard and felt.

All I ever wanted
was for her to protect
me from my demons.
Help me to slay them
when they came around.
All she did was become
one and I was left fighting
them again by myself.

She asked
if she could keep me?

So, I'm torn
as to why she
would ever let me go.

Her Colored Scars

I remember meeting you
and feeling like my soul
ran to you before my feet
even began to move.
I knew in that moment
I loved you.
I also knew you would
be the one to break me in half.
Still, my soul kept running.

You told me

not to fall in love with you.

Of course, I didn't listen.

Your love was

equivalent to quicksand.

Once I fell into it,

there would be no escaping.

I wish you
could've loved me
unafraid and without limits.
I hope you realize one day
what your heart is capable of.

I did it again.

I called you today

only for you not to pick up like always.

Unsteady and needing you to catch me,

I only kept falling.

It was the ground that caught my fall.

I will never understand why,

I keep thinking it will be you that catches me.

Her Colored Scars

It's always tempting
to me to return to her.
She's such a familiar acquaintance.
Her welcoming arms,
tender kisses and conversations.
I only ever come back for a visit though.
She doesn't know how
to properly entertain my heart.

Nothing was more important
behind closed doors than us.
In public, she was the only one
important.
That's what went wrong.

Her Colored Scars

I can write about you
until the world runs
out of ink and paper.
Still, it wouldn't be enough
to write out your memory.

J. A. Bishop

Your actions said

what your words couldn't.

You tried to hide your feelings

from me in fear of vulnerability.

So forgetful to know

that I could already see

everything in your eyes.

Her Colored Scars

Your tongue could break
me into a thousand of pieces
and I would still be yours.

Memories of you, creep through the corners of the box staring at me from the back of my closet. Unicorns and other animals from you that I once hugged to sleep all taped down in the box to keep the memories from sleeping around me.

Being loved
the same way twice,
is never bulletproof.
Some people can never
change even if they do
have all the love someone
can give them under one room.

Her body weighed

less on me than the

emptiness I felt letting her go.

Her Colored Scars

I didn't lie
when I said you
didn't hurt me.
Truth is,
you and your actions
nearly killed me.

J. A. Bishop

A later loss

would've been much worse.

Maybe that's why

I had to lose you now.

Her Colored Scars

They could bury me six feet under
and still you wouldn't know the
meaning of missing me.

Maybe one day

she would be dead to me.

Not in the way

that I could carry roses

to her grave,

but knowing of her

existence wouldn't hurt me anymore.

Her Colored Scars

Time is a killer
when you spend your day
staring at a clock.

I wear my poker face everyday

and I wear it well.

Even those around me

would never see

that I was falling apart on the inside.

Her Colored Scars

I've spent my life
chasing colored stones
and skipping them
in lakes with no depth.

Throw away the withered flowers
that you have collected between
each holiday of sweethearts.
You deserve fresh flowers, rooted
from the ground up.
Grown from tears of the rain
and love from the sunshine.

Her Colored Scars

Relationships
have taught me
that what you think is
solid gold only ends up
being sterling silver.

I lie in bed,

looking down at my hands.

Hands so small and very soft.

Reminiscing about how they've

had the pleasure to not only hold you,

but to touch you, rub you

from your head to your toes.

Thoughts so dirty, but so sad.

Good memories
have left a mark on me
more than the bad ones.
The bad ones, come and go.
However, it's the good ones
that keep me holding on.

J. A. Bishop

We only eat from boredom.

It feels us up and eliminates

time that we're wasting.

We just need to use our time better.

Do anything but sit

and indulge in constant gluttony.

Her Colored Scars

Dancing barefoot
to the rhythm of the rain,
is my favorite place
to try and forget you.

J. A. Bishop

I would've given you the moon,

but you only wanted a star,

something smaller less intricate.

Something that took less time to get.

If only you had patience,

one day you would've had

the whole night sky.

Her Colored Scars

I will forever
remember your
good days
of tending to
me on my days.
Kissing my
forehead to ease
my pain away.
Those days I wish
could've lasted forever.

J. A. Bishop

Pedal to the metal.

I hope you find what you're looking for.

Behind the steering wheel ready

to leave after breaking me down again.

I gave you more than you deserved

and in return I received less than I needed.

Like a doe in the headlights,

I'm frozen just to get a glimpse of you

before you run me over one last time.

How tragic is it
that I'm better at
breaking my own heart
than any other
human these days?

Ghosts of your past

always find their way

back to you

until you learn

what's keeping them here.

Her Colored Scars

Don't drown
Yourself in a
love that
you were
only meant
to dip your
feet into.

J. A. Bishop

Some women

live with the thought

that they might never

get the fairy tale ending.

Today, I am that woman.

And again,

I break the

promise to myself

not to fall for you.

J. A. Bishop

There was a storm
raging inside of me
that she caused
from her goodbye.
No one else knew why
dark clouds followed me
since the day she left.

Her Colored Scars

Half of my pain
was knowing I
couldn't fix
everything.

J. A. Bishop

She drove me
out of my mind most days,
but I would give anything
to be in her passenger seat
one last time.

The ground

is a hard

place to be

after someone

has swept

you off your feet.

It pains me to think

the last time you felt whole,

was when I held you.

Holding onto you

did more damage

to my hands

than a game

of tug-of-war.

I was holding onto

you so tightly

trying to love you

in all the ways

you were neglected.

I ended up suffocating you

and shattering you into ashes.

Don't waste your time
on someone who doesn't
cry for you the same way
you cry for them.

J. A. Bishop

My heart was far from neat.
It had been shattered
repeatedly through the years.
Faithfully put back together,
each piece holding on
with just a thread of hope.

Her Colored Scars

Looking through my eyes
wasn't for the faint of heart.
Even I have days
where I don't want
to look through them.

J. A. Bishop

You told me
I would find someone else if you left.
So confident that I would
have people knocking
down my door for a date.
You told me I would find better.
I thought you were reassuring me
of always having love.

How naïve I was,
not to know you were
just wishing me away.

Her Colored Scars

With each lie
you told,
you took my
soulful colors
and turned them to
different shades
of gray.

J. A. Bishop

I dreamed of you again last night.

I know this because I woke up

feeling like my heart had ran a marathon.

Us chasing each other

through fields of daises,

collapsing among the riverbanks

and sharing the moments

of our lives we have missed out on.

Its just a dream though and dreams end.

I'll have to wake up just to lose you again.

Goodbyes
always brought me
to a new hello until now.
I don't think I could handle
another familiar hello
or dragged out goodbye.

There was a sadness
in the way she looked at me
while I watched the snow
fall to the ground.
Almost as if she knew
both would soon be gone.

Her Colored Scars

I wish there was
a staircase to the sky
so, I could loan it
some of my tears,
for the sky hasn't
cried in days.

J. A. Bishop

How cruel would it be
to die in a world filled with
apathetic souls that were
just waiting for a
beating heart to make
them feel alive.

No one wants to cry
when someone leaves.
Still, people always leave,
and tears flow like rivers.

You didn't throw

away everything you had,

you only threw away me.

That was my mistake,

I thought I was your everything.

It gets hard to
breathe sometimes
knowing that
not breathing
takes a lot
less work.

Amazingly enough,
we're both looking
at the same sunset.
Sadly, we just happen
to be on two different rooftops
in different cities.

Is it your broken pieces
that scare you or the fact
that you don't feel compelled
to put the pieces together?

J. A. Bishop

I let my vinyl records spin
and close my eyes, so I can see
us dancing in my mind once again.
Your hand on my waist, my head on your chest.
If there was ever a dance number to dance
us out of my mind, this should be it.

Her Colored Scars

I was planning

for forever

while she was

planning for now.

We settle for

happily, ever never

when we couldn't agree.

J. A. Bishop

Her

Desires

J. A. Bishop

I crave for those experiences
the ones you read about
that take your breath away.
They make you want more.

The adventures that ignite
the very flame in your soul,
that you have no choice but
to go and explore our universe.

I never liked to wait
but I will if that's
what it takes to find
someone to awaken
the parts in me
that have been
dead for so long.

Love me

as a package or not at all.

Appreciate the intelligence that

flows through my mind

and feed it with your words.

Love me for my body,

every scar,

every inch and

every curve.

Appreciate what I'm letting you touch.

Love is what I love
and if doing
what I love kills me,
then I will die
loving every human
as much as possible.

I wonder if she too
looked at me like
all her questions
about love were
about to be answered.

She was like
the constellations.
You couldn't
look at her
without loving
the light
she provided
in the darkness.

J. A. Bishop

Hold onto the parts
of you that other
people whisper about.
Show me the crazy in you,
for anyone worth having
is worth a little craziness.

Her Colored Scars

Your name
will always live
in the darkest corners
of my mouth.
Ready to slip out
when I least expect it to.

Tonight, the moon creeps through my window blinds, an illuminating reflection of light against my skin. Lavender oil fills my room as I search for the perfect song to drift off to sleep. Longing for loves touch, settling for loves playlist.

Her Colored Scars

You wanted
to read me in chapters,
but I wanted someone
that was willing to
read me page by page,
word for word,
never skipping a beat
of learning who I was.

My lips left raw

after you kissed me

until midnight.

Offering you every inch

of my body knowing

that my lips couldn't take anymore.

Her Colored Scars

Her eyes could
start a fire,
burn cities to ashes
and set the most
beautiful forest
up in flames.
Even in her
destruction
the only thing
you will remember
is the sheet of colors
within her gaze.

J. A. Bishop

My heart falls for you
every season, like the
leaves hitting the ground.
Slowly falling never
knowing where ill end,
but still with the seasons
I fall for you every time.

Her Colored Scars

Today I am a sinner
seeking out exotic urges
to fulfill the passionate
thoughts that are kept within me.

Take me under you
like the sky over Georgia.
Touch me like you never
felt another humans touch.
You have me under your power
and tonight, we'll be burning
brighter than any flame.

Her Colored Scars

Love me
starting with
my scars,
those are
what will lead
you to my heart.

The night is young,

let yourself live a little.

See what the other side is like.

Come with me to the wild side.

Let your wildness run free.

A one-way ticket

to a heart with no

intentions of a return,

that must be what a

sense of security

in love feels like.

It was addictive.

Your lips that tasted

like alcohol mixed

with a lingering taste of honey.

I never wanted to get drunk with anyone,

but with you, your honey always

found its way to my soul.

How could

I hate someone

that I still wish

could reach out to me?

J. A. Bishop

They were sirens,

under a spell I was

listening to their song.

Intentions of seducing

and destroying me,

but never to fall in love.

I overthink my need for you.
The sound of your voice,
craving your body and
longing for your love.
I don't need you,
I want you.

Her love shook me

like an earthquake on the west coast.

It was scary at times,

it cracked the ground beneath us

and was unpredictable.

Nonetheless, a little tremor

was worth her love.

What is living

without skinny dipping

on a cool July night

with the water brushing

against your bare body.

Let me be that fantasy for you.

The one you day dream about.

The one you can't have because

you know it will turn you into

a better person.

Her Colored Scars

I was everything
in living color
that you didn't know
your black and white
life needed.

All I want is someone that's not afraid

to touch the wounds, she left behind.

Someone not afraid to get their hands dirty

or ask how the wounds got there.

Someone not scared to know my past.

Show me

that not all covers.

have the same inside.

Some people have left
my heart in pieces.
Sent my life up in sparks
and had me hunting desires
instead of chasing my dreams.

Give me honesty
and faithfulness.
A full night
of conversation
that drives the
passion out of me.

Collapse into me

and let our worries

fall to our feet,

cascading over us

like a waterfall.

Let the ripples

wash away our fears,

doubts and insecurities

until we feel serenity

between our bodies.

Today I woke up
knowing that you
just weren't ready
for a love as big as mine.
Yet, I still haven't figured
out how not to love you.

Your love blinded me

like the sunrise

on early morning walks

along the beach.

I never worry though,

just like the moon

you always lure me back in.

Her Colored Scars

Please understand

that even silence

is a desirable trait

that we all should possess.

In your absence

I wanted to thrive

for a better me that I once lost.

I wanted my eyes to light up

when I talked about my life,

the way they did when

I use to talk about you.

Her Colored Scars

Some nights
I wish you could
sleep walk your
way back to me.
Sneak into my bed,
faithfully hold
me until morning.

I will always be a dreamer

pulling up daises and looking for answers.

Do you love me, do you love me not?

Petals get pulled and it's never the answer I want.

I fall harder than rain
during an April shower
when love is involved.

J. A. Bishop

Rain beating down on a tin roof,

droplets hitting my

bedroom window pane.

Us in a state of comfort

in this bed that I have made,

your flesh and my fantasies.

Yeah, that would be enough

to make angels cry.

Let your heart beat
for the things you love,
if it can't beat for someone
you have yet to meet.

J. A. Bishop

Some want the family,

the husband or wife,

the white picket fences

lined with azaleas.

For me, I'm just living

to make the young

12-year-old me happy.

Her Colored Scars

Maybe just for tonight
you can be mine
and make me
believe in love again.

J. A. Bishop

Don't give me

a forever kind of love

give me a Sunday kind.

The kind where the world

is turned off and only you and I exist.

Her Colored Scars

Girls with tattoos
and egotistical ways
were always the
sweetest temptation for me.

J. A. Bishop

A sprinkle of sugar

on my tongue use to

justify my taste of sweetness

until I pressed my tongue against

you and tasted something much sweeter.

Her Colored Scars

A smile can bring
many feelings to surface,
cause a lot of tension
to build and make you forget
all the pain that once was there.

J. A. Bishop

She captured my heart

simply by being herself.

No extra layers of makeup,

no need for an extra voice

telling her what to do.

I fear women today,

don't know how to do that.

Touch my soul in
ways your hands
never could.
Leave an
imprint on my mind
like a passage from
your favorite book.

Under a blanket

of stars and darkness,

seduce me.

While everyone in the city

is sleeping,

let my cries of pleasure

be a call to the lovers in the world.

Bury yourself into me,

while you rock me back to sleep.

Her Colored Scars

In my

darkest days,

I spoke love

into existence.

Like a secret

that couldn't be kept

behind sealed lips.

I still wait for you,

for the love that's

suppose to find me.

J. A. Bishop

I only want to wake up

to see her silhouette

standing in front of me.

Sunlight beaming on

her poised bare body

with her hair sweeping

down her back, while she

looked back at me with

pleading eyes to bring her back to bed.

A poisonous apple

to my soul,

you would leave me

under a spell

with just one bite.

J. A. Bishop

Hurricanes are my choice

for lovers even though

they only bring storms

to my heart instead of the bedroom.

Delivering madness and neglecting

me of passion.

So give me a hurricane

for a lover, for I've learned

how to weather those storms.

Her Colored Scars

My neck wasn't fitted
for black chokers.
I just needed her hands
around my throat
making me fall to my
knees at her mercy.

Explore me

like your favorite hideaway

beneath the sheets.

Breathe me in

and let me envelop you

in the most intimate ways.

Her Colored Scars

Between the
beautiful smile
and piercing eyes
there were secrets
I was longing to know.

J. A. Bishop

Tell me what

you mean with words,

just say it. If it's too hard to say,

tell me with your touch, just touch me.

Her Colored Scars

Much like
the moon,
I would like
to hold you
with both hands
to feel your imperfections.

J. A. Bishop

My expectations
set my desires up in flames.
I was only looking for happiness
and what I found was disappointment.

The End

Gratitude

To my mom, thank you for listening to my dreams and supporting me on the journey to making all of them come true. Thank you for all that you do for me in life. I am forever in debt to you.

To my best friend and cousin since youth, Crystal. Without you these poems would just be random words written on pages in my notebooks. Thank you for not only pushing me everyday to keep focus on this dream of mine to publish "Her Colored Scars" but helping me to edit my book.

To Christy, thank you for being one of my biggest supporters. I appreciate you more than you will ever know. Thank you for letting me bounce book ideas off you and for cheering me on through this process.

To anyone else, that has helped me and supported me with this book, thank you.

About the author

Jennifer Bishop is a writer based between Georgia and South Carolina. She shares her writing in hopes to create a safe place for women around the world that need a place to rest their hearts. She writes from experience of life, love, heartbreak and loss. When she is not writing she can be found doing yoga or getting lost under the sun, between the trees.

Made in the USA
Middletown, DE
30 January 2019